Fieldnotes

Mark Weiss

Fieldnotes

Junction Press
San Diego
1995

 Cover art by Charles Burchfield, "Moon Through Young Sunflowers," courtesy of the Carnegie Museum of Art, Pittsburgh, Pennsylvania (Gift of Mr. and Mrs. James H. Beal).

The author wishes to thank Ira Beryl Brukner, Marc Kaminsky, Pamela Portwood and Mac Wellman, fine editors all, for their rigorous and generous readings of the manuscript of this book in its various incarnations.

Library of Congress Catalogue Card Number: 94-07815
ISBN:1-881523-04-7
JunctionPress POBox 40537 San Diego CA 92164-0537

Solo

Coasting down the mountain to gas
and a slow food stop. Across the road
a horse show.
In the mountains of West Virginia.

.

St. Albans–
sternwheeler pushing barges down the Kanawha.

.

Street fair–Kentucky.
Hot dogs and pretty girls.

.

In the morning light the land
looks tacky.
60 miles to Kansas.

.

You drive 600 miles, get out
to stretch your legs and they talk
a foreign language. Missed–
the interstices.

.

The cooking
longer than
the eating.

.

Otto's Cafe, Pittsburgh, Kansas
the businessmen at breakfast, bisquits and gravy,
assess the calamity. All the farms

gone. Across the street
the dead hotel, the whole of Main Street empty.

.

Field guide to highway cops.

.

Booze.
Toilet paper.

.

Marplot, as thunder storm,
bowls in from the west. Looking south
through the open door where clouds
are sunlit and slate, and the ragged edge of a
pine-covered slope–black
as shadow against the mountain behind it. Lightning. Again.
Thunder. And the sheen
of rain in the street
and a yellow truck, and a red
matchbook flapping on the tarmac. A man
sunlit   in plaid shirt
jeans
and a railroad cap
walks in the rain eating green ice-cream, and the girl in the
            doorway
across the way eats pink.
Lightning. Pink
to the west, and lavender. Get wet
watching sunset, eager
to swallow it.

.

First day in the mountains camped 4 miles west of Cripple Creek–9000 feet. Alternating sun and thunder storms. Watching the weather roll in.

This afternoon coming up from the prairie I circled a storm–that clearly defined. The air so dry that a lot of rain never makes it–you see it leave the cloud–thick grey mass, thinning to wisps, then nothing. The prairie parched, bleached, broken by dry water-courses. Up here,

moist and lush. Breathing a small effort, and a walk around town takes some determination. Up and down the mountain. A main

street of substantial Victorian buildings–1880s-1910–the rest of the town small gingerbreads, scattered, as if thrown from a dice cup. A mining town, once 40,000, now a revived ghost town. Victor, the next town over and 1000 feet higher, smaller and more sedate. Lots of antique stores. And three active goldmines.
Coming across uneventful. Hot. Lexington looks a nice town. Witchita doesn't seem to have a center. Leaving there, the man in the camera store said, "the route you're taking, there's nothing to see." "That's what I came for," I told him.
From Poplar Grove, Missouri, through the Ozarks, then across Kansas, the land rises in terraces, almost imperceptibly, and the vegetation changes, and the climate, and the way people work and build their houses, until finally there are no trees except the groves shading the ranchhouse and its outbuildings–how they must have been tended–and the growth along the rivers, such as they are at this season, and
suddenly all along looking for them the excitement growing, palpable–suddenly–well above the horizon the mountains–remnants of snow–shining, growing, as you get closer. 100 miles away first seen, halfway between Lamar and Pueblo.
A Mexican meal in Pueblo, then drive due west to Florence, a few streets of good houses in the bottom of a large arroyo. North from there on a dirt road, Phantom Creek Canyon, 4,000 to 10,000 feet, one lane wide, red rock canyon, wildflowers: chapparal–almost desert, becoming pines, grasses and aspens. Stand in the cold
ankle-deep water
and think this
is what I came for, this is what I drove
2000 miles for. Only the sounds of birds
breeze
and the water flowing.

Alone these four days
eyes aching with the constant sun-glare–
shaking with fatigue–
12, 14 hours of high-speed driving a day, sorting out my life,
nostalgic for Joan, and realize
the last time I did this drive was with her, appreciating her
careful silence. Well. Perhaps a mistake.

It goes like this. First day
singing with the freedom of being alone   second day
missing Joan   third day, thinking
it might be nice to have a mate.
A careful
quiet mate. But today
in the mountains
at dusk
the tips of the long grasses
float, flaxen, above the meadow's green. Two kids
make noise in a stream and along the stream-bed.
Everything greener.

.

Cairo, where Huck and Jim
made a wrong turn,
a ghost town.
Only Paducah.
The meeting of waters.
Flat, humid, the head of the delta
a channel once to the Gulf of St. Lawrence.

.

60 miles of flat cropland to the first
terrace of the Ozark Plateau.

.

Running with a thunderstorm across Kansas.

.

While the last of the afterglow still
silhouettes the mountains
a great black cloud covers the sky. Only Venus,
first and only,
low in the sky.

.

I sit on my tent's small–
call it–apron,
cross-legged, facing
the lantern.

.

Large breaks in the cloud-cover,
so that a few stars show through. In the distance

a man wields an axe.
Small cones in the duff
where I will certainly stand,
hard on bare feet. No two
alike.

.

Too small
even to be seen.

.

The ant in my tent thinks,
"oh my god,
the habitation of humans."

. . .

How long
how many days of silence
before the ringing of civilization is stilled.

.

At once
grateful for company and
disappointed. Outside,
mountains. Wind takes the tent
like a sail   the stars
themselves seem to blow past. I write
silently as possible, grateful
for the silent pen. Inside
the spiral of this nebula,
inside my silence.

.

Such a mess of stars,
like lint, my friend says. Stars,
nothing but stars.

.

The wet
tongue of a large black dog.

.

Slow ooze of water on the slate
floor of the irrigation ditch as the train rounds
the curve in my dream on the way
to the mansion, where I will be
an unfit guest, nonetheless
moves me as if I also
were restored to fruitfulness. "You look
like you're losing control
of this thing," says the giant
hand as it closes the door.

.

The large white car from the twenties.
She wants me to find our trunks, but I'm writing a poem.
She's worried about appropriate dress and behavior, but the
hosts
are concerned to take care of everything.

.

A hand
holds my book up,
as if to say,
"write."

One rises sometimes
to the surface of sleep.

Even in sleep I make choices.

.

Pattern through time.

.

Outside of Albuquerque
far from home.

.

Full rainbow and its reflection over Winslow, Arizona. One
street
in each direction.

Everybody says the Apaches get lots of rain. "You don't
want to go to the movies, it's all
Indians." "What does that mean? I'm not from here."

"This is a drunk area. Stay home and watch tv."

"What we got here is dust."

.

Winslow beseiged. Don't know why they keep her.

.

Fat-bellied storm cloud
over the ponderosas.
Mogollon Rim.

.

Red penstemon.

.

Biochemical restlessness.

"I'm a long time travellin
here below..."

.

The men confer
the kid
pets the dog.

.

Invoke his name
and it happens again.

.

Small volcanoes south of Hopi.

.

Bewildered by the passage of time.
Sky-shredding tower in the Pinaleños.
Ore-trucks with Idaho plates.

.

She was troubled to think of the grown man in her son's bed. Why
had she put him there?

.

Claiming the guest.

.

Purple hair
sallow skin   she thinks
that loneliness is the whole problem.

.

All of these faces with one nose.

.

The tenderness of the desert.

A lizard   fast as a shadow
runs across the bare ground. A hawk
follows me, perching on each phone pole.
A dove nests in the groin of a cactus.

.

I open the curtains to let in the night.

.

Sun-bleached, and a few oranges.

.

Very quietly the accident
assumes its permanence.

.

Spider dies   and all those flies
wasted.

.

"It's not pretty," the oleander, "it
grows here." "Don't get out of the car
between here and Yuma."

.

"I'm very straight-forward," she says,
and grabs my shirt.

.

She shows him a nipple. He strokes her thigh. They know I'm
watching.

.

Is this the big one? Do I rush for the doorway? Will the house
slide down the mountain?
Do I put on my pants?

.

Hours watching the shadows,
taking note.

.

Arrested in motion
by a girl's voice

across the valley.

.

A fog takes the city.

Has taken the city.

Fragrant with desert and ocean.

.

Stands on one leg,
falls over.

Has gotten used to silence.

.

This bull has had no experience,
till now,
of failure.

.

And removed the sword
so that he could die.

.

This is the letter that I never sent from a three-month's
journey.
I am bronzed
and fat
and inhabit the land.
The sparse desert, doves, saguaro,
palo verde
blond cholla and the anxious
ground-huggers,
lizards and centipedes.
Silence. The flutter of wings. The kestrel's
quick shadow.

.

The anticipation of solitude
is solitude.

To be alone with.

Tiptoeing around in a stranger's house–

ill-at-ease,
breathlessly so.

The sound of the thunder could be an earthquake.

That I love
what has been more than
what is, keeping the ghost
of it close to me.

.

A trained imagination
blinded by wonder, momentum,
and the shape of motion.

.

Paradise
is warm weather. No irony
in paradise.
A clean
statement.

.

I buy expensive things from
prosperous merchants, while all around me mothers
and children beg
or offer a handful of penny-candies
to keep from starving. I give them nothing
and buy nothing.

.

Their eyes, the children's
sleepy laughter.

.

The boys fight
for the pillows in the bull-ring. It's a
desperate game. I think of the bull, stunned and
panting, exhausted suddenly by the picador's blade. The rest
is automatic: the bull,
already done for, does
what it must, the matador
also.

A dirty business for everyone.

.

“Without the sky there would be no mother.”

.

The book of wonders.
As if this were an unknown place.
Even with the guidance of the elders a country
without history.
Without history
in this place. Scabby
varicolored growth of iceplants on the hills,
a slough
of skin like a shedding snake. So,
reptilian. A thing to know. A first
step.
Large stretches
of cactus and other
thorned things   scorpions
fire ants   deadly spiders. In paradise
it never rains. In paradise
there is no irony. Unclouded eyes
of the onlookers.
Tired children in the bordertown,
dusty-eyed,
barefoot,
flogging penny-candies
into midnight.

.

She was closing shop when he came by. She stepped
halfway out, holding the door
with her foot. “You back
to stay?”

.

When he’s away from home,
a dog’s wild-life.

.

Wind and rain had woven their pattern into the duff.

.

White gull on roller skates.

Everything as if seen for the first time.

.

Good-humored, complex
self-sufficient men.

.

The young mother pulls up the left side of her black sweater
to nurse, then covers herself with
a blanket for the sake of modesty. It slips; holding it
with her teeth, she pauses in thought.
She has red hair
and turqoise eyes.

.

The work   of a man's hand.

The immigrant's distance.

Sturdy Protestant clutter.

Turn off the light to look at the darkness.

.

By the monument to the Holocaust
small orange blossoms on
fragile green stems
open a vortex.

.

Foam around the cliffs
a line of white   flat
grey water. The life
or the artifice, dead grass,
seed and stalk,
made signal when the word says,
"There!" Forever noted.

.

The moon emerges and does
for the moment
illuminate the water.

.

Glimpsed three white galleries away
the skinny brunette in expensive red I have studied

this hour and more, angular
in the oversized doorways.
As if seen through mirrors.
As if aged.
High heels,
mottled legs,
taut as a greyhound. But the eyes
of a wary child. Her hands, red-nailed,
claw-like, and her wedding ring.
Banded.
She could tear at her meat,
devour
it, blood-lipped, and never
break free. Down the corridors
the echo of wings.

.

"Save the bones
for Henry Jones."

.

Great granite hump of the mountain.
Silence, to
hold onto solitude.

.

The sun's reflection travels the rails.

.

Twitter of bats and cicadas.
And the fear of animals.

.

A pull, a tug
downwards, a vortex, and the sky
drowned in moonlight, the moon
afloat
in its own
viscous light.
In itself.

.

Tent swimming in moonlight   moon
low in the sky,
silhouettes of pine trees.

Later:
moon down   very dark.

.

A drop of water
lost among the hairs.

. . .

Cruising north by moonlight.

.

Two black dogs raise dust, eat sunset.

.

The woodsman's axe
determines treeline.
Last pink light
sliding up the canyon.

.

Sliding down the tail of the Bear.
Stars   as if windblown.

.

The tribe of women. "They asked us,"
the messenger said, "to come along with them
and have their children for them."

.

To have an erotic dream about your mother
after all this time.

.

I'm new on this planet.

.

All the white hours
as betokened by a blowing cloth
to close the door and an
open fence beyond it.

.

A chicken
with a mind of its own. "That chicken

had its own reasons."

.

What he sees
when he looks
is the hang
of fabric–character,
class
and intonation. "Makes
the man"
as much as any gesture.

But it's what he sees.

.

All things made human by the eye and hand.
See how the scratches in the pictured sky
become the cracked fabric of grief and power
that all flee from. Guns,
and the hands that wield them.

.

Where the paper was stretched,
waiting for silence to do its business.

.

This heavy white crockery
white sink
smooth water. Wanting
to put one foot
in front of another. Look,
last night I saw a doe
not thirty feet away in the high brush of this remnant prairie.
            She
made no sound
though she bounded away
leaping five feet
and landing soundlessly
not even disturbing the grass. It must have been her movement
that made me turn to watch her, woke
me.

.

The traffic of the first ten feet of air.

.

What must be done overwhelms intention.

.

Green sweater, red hair
and terrified,
holding a pickle.

.

Fixed
to the actual,
so that I missed my turn.

.

This is the what that gets remembered.

.

In dreams and recollections
as palpable as any actor.

.

When the convenience of each depends upon
the concern of all.

.

What is it that I don't remember
not having known before?

.

The year of my father's birth
his brother died. My father
used to talk to him
to ask his help
to intervene
between him, his mother's need
and his father's violence. His father
used to dance the *czardas*
all night long at parties. In the twilight of streetlamps
he thrashed on the bed
his heart collapsing
while my father ran for help.
There was never help.
In the *shul* where the rich prayed
they fed my father table scraps
in return for songs.

In the year of my birth
his father died,
a florid man
of few satisfactions
and no past.
And my father will have no grandsons.

.

All night long the glorious wind
and occasional showers.

.

So many discoveries, but forced to sleep. The moth
bangs at the lampshade. Outside
the full breezes of evening have given way
to the steady rain that will fall all night and
into tomorrow. "An autumn storm"
across the prairie. Would stay awake
to hear it.

.

A voice   charged with static,
as if all that electricity
had nowhere to go.

.

He makes a theatrical gesture, turns
and walks away, pretending
he'd forgotten something. But he'd only wanted
to see the girl.

.

A trick of reflection makes her image float
on the surface of the glass
before she enters. Strange,
he thinks, she had seemed
completely serene, that surface, but the girl
in the doorway now pouts
as if she always pouted.

.

A clod of earth of suspicious nature.

.

The inky stain of a mushroom that
consumes itself in its own

juices is
on my shoe, where I
poked it, as if
it were an animate,
poisonous thing.

.

Deep, peevish, glandular memory.

.

The moon-inflicted night.

.

The moon in its passing burns the clouds, and the star
passes through clouds, emerges
gemlike.
In his head
pictures of other places.

.

More interested in comfort than symmetry.

.

A large crow walks the lawn, pecking at
whatever's
to eat.

.

Even the little souls of the grass, she said,
even those.

.

Walking out   in the pale
fragrant rain, the bare
fragrant rain.

Has the rain
stopped, and are there stars?

.

One drop of water hangs
from the bottom of each
red fruit of the hawthorn.

.

No organizing principle,
then, no intelligence.
Don't expectorate   *défense*

de cracher–spreads germs,
"bugs" (invisible insects) attack
the blood, the brain,
the balls. "I want
to vomit
when you do that."

.

The tongue finds it, and the mind
blinded.

.

I study threeness.
Folds back on itself.

.

May the watercourses turn to stone in your cities.

.

Where the air
left it.
Here, as in this dream,
there was a flat surface.
Dead toad bloats in the sun, drowned worms,
the insects recovering,
complaining birds,
slugs.

.

Or more,
the act of cutting cuts both ways.

.

Discovery of the lost father.

.

Exploring the unexamined life.
Picking the bones of narrative.
So many bricks
polished by the misfortunes of bricks.

.

Mobility defines the child.
What kind of a man would plant thorns
on his mother's grave?

Waves

In the quest the rider on the grey horse
disappears into the swirling white   cold horse
cold rider.
Or maybe it's a pale car
that's seen better days,
heater on the fritz.

In motion   as it's always
in motion.

.

Its tongue   like an arrow   searches the undergrowth.

.

The satisfactions of birds.

.

Wiping a piece of dust from your picture
as if picking a hair from your lip.

.

As if to turn away
were to be invisible.

.

If myth is metaphor through time it's walking
the border,
the boundary-walker.
After you tell the one story. After,
you tell
the one story.

.

The vague idea of a consort.
In the war with the ants
prince of the wee-folk.

.

Carrying her own shadow in hand,
training her shadow.

.

Lost hold of the tail of language.

.

Each loss the first loss.
Willing the time to pass quickly.
Nervous gestures, the tearing of paper. The telephone
white,
silent.

.

By now she's waking up
holding her lover
greeting the cat.
Her feet are on the floor by now she walks
to the shower her long
body glides upwards through the water,
gets out, shivers,
puts color
under her eyes and on her cheeks,
does her lashes,
dresses,
and goes to work.

.

Searching for the thread that leads outwards.

.

The harsh grass of a dry place.
The russet among the wheat.

.

I am your worst fears come to light
I am the night

I am the dark place beneath the stone.

.

Under the hill.

Under the ivy.

.

Moon riding the black back of the wave.
At rest in the shallows.

.

The eye begins to articulate night.
A gull among the ducks.

.

A duck   and another duck.

.

The fierce sheep that ride the surf.

.

It was dangerous
sometimes to swim
in that lake the fish
bit at their nipples.

.

The crowd
of knights and ladies
descending into the earth and all.

.

The great glow to the west that wipes out the stars.
In that quadrant the city,
80 miles away,
more powerful than night.

.

Three doves feed from a tray on the lawn,
fly off as I pass.

.

Dandelions and white clover by the side of the road.

.

Three deformed cygnets, each
with its right leg folded over its back. They manage to swim,
        but will never
be airborne. Gonners by winter. Their parents
magisterial, perfect.

.

Encouraging the spiders,

discouraging the deer-flies.

.

Bog-laurel, deep
deep pink
with purple eyes, one
to a petal,
five in all, each blossom
a small
scalloped cup
in the scalloped vase that my love gave me on the bureau
beneath the painting of a woman
offering a drink
to a blue bird. In the night
in the small forest beyond the next houses
the whole understory
bog-laurel   the rustle of twigs in the welcome breeze.
Nothing but night between her and me.
Between here and there.

.

When for a moment
the two songs come together.

.

The swan's hiss.
The rustle of leaves.

.

The swift beak of a skimmer as it beats the shore.

.

Making
different kinds of peace
at each hour.

.

A small bug circles its shadow. Then
it appears to carry its shadow on its back.

Large burden
for a small bug.

.

Irony is the exile's deformity.

.

In exile among the ducks.

.

The crowds the waves
the terrifying laughter of gulls.

.

Fucking with the generative principle.

.

Storm coming in   in the distance
lightning.
Midnight. My shadow on the beach a giant
ungainly presence,
arms at its sides,
walking towards the waves.

.

Listen to the voice
humming within me.

.

The woman reminds him of someone what was
her name and he realizes it was a girl he had loved once,
whose name he had lost.

.

In place of the promised storm
a fine, quiet wind into morning, my bed
tending to its usual chaos.

.

All night the air
almost sickly with honeysuckle
and the scent of grass. In the dark,
gliding through it   my bike
whirring patiently, the smell
as palpable as light.
Steering   by the sky   just visible
between the trees.

.

This or that spotted stone.

.

Followed by the fog.

.

Worked by the waves.

.

Asking the language to do new things.

.

The young girl, dazed
by the eyes of men   so many glances
to find an answer for.

.

Like joyless children.

.

What a pleasure your hands are!

.

The web of muscle and skin
connecting thumb to hand.

.

The wind freshens
and lightning
to the west.
A low groan.
A few stars.

Despite the screens, my cottage
a wilderness of small insects.

.

Up to my thighs in bay-water,
feet in the muck,
looking for clams. The low shore
the flat landscape
the fat blue sky.
A pair of skimmers overhead, unique among birds
for their lower lip, and a duck in the distance,
in for a landing.

.

The windsurfer, her back to me, again and again
hauls up the sail.

.

The laborious flight of a swan. By the pond
the corpse of a gull,
beaten and drowned. Around it,

the cob's feathers.
By afternoon the ants have begun their work.

.

A second spider in my bed, as if
the messenger of lightning.

.

In the shallows, a horseshoe crab
with a mane of algae.

.

Invented night.
Black   and a black-bird, dead,
beneath the bush at the edge of the lawn where a cat
perhaps had left it. Seen,
and told.

.

There are now three spiders
and a great many moths.
Big one, smaller, smallest.
My door is always open.

.

I destroy
only those
that land on me.

.

A drop of water like a metronome, then stops,
then starts again.

.

Clotted foam sliding down the beach.

.

Down to the inlet to look at the moon. An egret
floats over the fog and is
gone.

.

The black dog riding the waves.

.

All night the ducks complain.
Four of them float
across the moon.
First bullfrogs of summer,

none too soon.

.

Turtle feels my shadow
and plunges. Many turtles.

Trees and the reflections of trees.

The moon and its shadows.

.

The voice of consciousness like the hum of blood
in a total silence.

.

Slow gathering,
shard by shard,
handful of seed,
the field unsorted.
Squint-eyed. Rye barley
ragweed corn
plantain-grass clover.

.

Small cottage grey shakes
door always open screen door
for the flies. A sickly birch
an old red
picnic table with bench and stools the same covered with
 shells and stones
on a red
brick patio in front of the door. Inside,
a bed a table dresser
shelves another table for the computer
a fridge a microwave a range a sink.
Sliding doors. Bathroom and closet.
A shower stall.
Many spiders. Carpeting. Three pictures.
Two lamps. Five small high windows with blinds or curtains.
Tight ship
if a storm should come.

.

So long to find my solitude.

Long enough
that her presence
became my solitude.

.

Tattered wings of the gull–storm-struck
or combat? The sea
breaks higher today after three
incessant days of storm. To the west
where the winds come from,
under purple and grey ochre,
denoting fair weather.
Men in baseball caps hold small children and talk.
Sandy contentment.
All urgency drained from the act,
while as though the bulls of Poseidon continue their attack on
the beach,
reshaped in the night. I sit
at the edge of the surf where surf was yesterday,
the crest of the wave broken to spray
by its fierce momentum and the implacable
intractable
slow drift of sandbars.

.

Supposing a fish.

.

Taxed with the luck of the human.

.

Evening glorious
with mimosas and the flights of swallows.

Moon twitters in the branches.

.

Humility of other people's dreams.

.

The aborted gesture. And beyond,
the trees.
One butterfly across the tennis court.

The pong of the ball.

.

She saw me watching her watch herself
and turned away.

.

One bright planet to the south
and another to the east,
sky full of stars. Dark,
until the eye,
and the grass dew-thickened
where the grass is, in a place
said to be dangerous.

.

As a matter of fact,
they weren't laughing at her.

.

Feathers of a black bird.

.

Scallop shards
cleanly broken at the growth-ring.

Fragments of a lost iconography of stripes.

What meaning can anything have outside the context of these
colors?

Sea-froth seething, and bubbles at the margin.
The sand churning into cliffs and canyons.

A gull's wing turned to nostalgia by the actions of wind and
wave.

The music seen thus clearly
despite the flies.
Outside of all engagement with human life,
despite a sudden sympathy for the fat families and their sandy
offspring. If I could lift this weight.
If I could find the treasure-box hidden beneath the breakwater
40 years ago

before the great bull bellowed its threats quite so loud as now.

.

Starlings going crazy in the one tree at sunset.

.

"She moves
from one crisis to another. Her life's
like that."
Pain.
Attendant nausea.

.

Everywhere the rich
aspire to cleanliness.

.

"Go"–urinate, "come"–orgasm,
"go"–evacuate, "come"–
arrive at a new place.

.

Light penetrating to the deepest forest,
to the last
low tree.

.

I have warmed your place.

.

The behavior of animals in crowded cages.

.

Rewarded
for a long walk
by a sail
that's caught the sunset where the mountains
drop to the sea.
The ghost of an island southward.

.

The miraculously preserved nipple of the Virgin.

.

A voyage to a *white space.*

Improvised,

as is the light.

The structure, or at least
the process
of improvisation

to travel
in search of the light, as if
sampling   tasting

chasing it.

Even the sky in patches

as if there were depth to the water.

.

Raped by her brother sun, the moon

Refusing the easy comforts

the arbitrary and implacable facts. Look,
today the beach assumes its cliff-aspect
and the cannibal sheep attack the sand in a landscape
where the only bright colors are poison.

.

Looking
and doing.

.

The hierarchy of sensation.

.

Wed to trajectory.

.

Cn ah have a dollah
fo rice and beans?
Beaming. *Ah loves*
rice and beans.
And chomps
her toothless gums.

.

That happened to other people.

.

Herding their animals between winter and summer.

.

Wondering if the noise is thunder or gunfire.

It all goes down, is
going down.

.

Before nouns

before verbs

chaotic reach of a single tree

the southern limit of maples
in the unpredictable changes of seacoast climate, currents
heat-driven

replace the dying with a date-palm. Central Park
the peaceable kingdom
according to

rain, and the dark stain of the water
turning the asphalt purple.

That terror is your only strength.

You will always have access to the terror now.

Artifacts:
40 Poems

I

As I was down walking on

Not to be shy in the face of

Grief
not wants to eat, but well-fed should,
well-fed!

At night   the light
on the water?

II

1
Firmly, but kindly,
as if speaking
to a well-behaved child.

2
A turn in
the dance that seemed
a bond, an
anchor. Wing
dipping to its own reflection.

Between a man and a woman
brocade of hands,
branches.

3
Expression. Won't flex?

Cast of face

Smell of wet leather

Gestures of forgetfulness

Forgeries.

Symmetry as an excuse for being.

The cost, the cost
of

4
Squat, squat like
a frog,
squat
squat.

To engage
pelvis, bowels
the heels of both feet.

Empty, like a tunnel. *"I feel*
like a tunnel," wind,
polyps.

III

Reach out   to the detail
so as not to get lost. So,
maps on the table-cloth.
This place, too,
could be a juncture.

And the arrow of purpose,
the will to kill,
as if the broken shell revealed
another shell, as in
"it's turtles all the way
Dr. James."

IV

1
She waters her face, in the morning
she waters her face
and sits in a closet.

2
Swan-like, and claims
an extra vertebra.

V

"Guaranteed destruction of confidential records."

Reflections.
Pieces.

Enamored
of an odd cast of face.

A lot of shouting at recalcitrant cows.

He thinks the gulls are ducks. "Poor ducky,"
he says.

The truth is
she was a fearful woman
and did much to hide it.

Of whom nothing survives but the reputation.

Many things are not seagulls.

A certain fracturing of sound.

The lovely hiss of lizards, then,
among the leathery foliage.

VI

She was annoyed by their constant evaluations   on street
            corners,
at the foot of stairs,

To preserve the adolescent's sense of his own importance.

The cycle of history according to Time-Life.

Sepia skin. Ukrainian, I think. Flesh
freighted with history.

VII

A questioning tongue.

The knife must be sharp, and the cutter skillful.

VIII

There are always outlyers in a flock of pigeons. Today
one of them, wind-held, poises quite motionless as the flock
wheels around him.

·

Important to note that the sky
was grey and luminous.

·

Hung like an ornament.

·

Like an emblem.

IX

Just before spring
and the ghosts of trees on the Palisades.

Driving across the shadows of bare branches.

Through the shadows of bare branches.

All these things that should never have happened.

"Charlotte is the mother because,
she tells the others, she is wearing the silver shoes."

X

Chill, fragrant, penetrated with water.

Red nodes on the rosebush.
To fertilize.

Said to be beautiful.
Her hands embrace.
Her hands' embrace.
Blue jeans, and purple gloves.
Clouds, as if generated. In a sheltered place
magnolias   and the astonishing green eyes
of a girl glimpsed
as she passed on a bicycle   not seen
except her eyes.

Corner on the wonder market.
They discuss
cuckolding her husband. He passes
the restaurant they sit in. "Oh, there's John,"
she says, "sucking an ice-cream." They beat on the plate-glass
to get his attention. He glances their way
without enthusiasm, and she explodes
with laughter.

Oh gee   look at me

pain   and his children.

She squints   her whole face
a squint.

No sooner   no later
despite the shaking.

Making an appearance before the world
practicing her welcome strut.

Women
wearing leotards
jumping up and down.

Red hair
orange tears.

Walking the platform.
Copping a look.

Mistress of the apprehensive glance.

Every golden cloud must be weighted with lead
he said.

When the gull
crosses the path of light and becomes golden.

Lost in the tailspin
astonished and curious to know
that this is it,
and relieved also.

Unrolled her tongue like a lizard
stalking a fly.

XI

1
To become transparent.

A hand becomes a slap.

But the lamb is dead regardless.

2
To learn more about human suffering than I could have,
growing up in a grave.

Some sort of correspondence between hands and feet.

Pale hair of evening.
Pale hair of morning.

The heft of a shell.

3
On the subway
soft breast against my chest.
Look bored so as not to frighten her.

No eye-contact.

Statues in their purple shrouds.

The unexpected bitterness of the day.

Either a shadow
or a scar.

4
In a dream
two girls feed me parsley.

Isn't it lovely   the blur of faces.

XII

Say it
directly. The man of joy
the man of grief
and a picture of carnival masks.

Head against belly
listening to
the double rhythm of breath and blood.

"In a flat country," he said,
build square cities."

XIII

Not the bird
but its shadow
falls from the sky.

Rebuild a mountain
to get her back.

"Over the modulations of the wind
I could hear the faint sounds of leaf crunching
from the dark rider above me."

XIV

One little stitch in the eyelid
to keep it shut.
Dry mango seed on a wooden table
among the cutlery and the clatter of dishware. White,
shiny, with a dark blue line
like a horizon or a tide-line on the
broken saucer. Heavy with its
own substance,
weight, and a chalky
edge–texture, and a cutting edge. The lake
breaks into light and dark
in a hole in the table.
There are no people here. There will not
be people here.
Under the lid
an eye
swims toward the light like a large
wet moth.

XV

1
Do you live near a smelter?
Is the pottery you eat on glazed with lead?

2
We call the echo "mockery."

3
Did you braid your teeth?
Did you wet your wife?

4
On the other side
a different set of shadows.

No place
without its season of bugs
or the like.

XVI

1
I do not ask you to stop kicking my body.
I think and say
even what I think and say.

2
Batteries.
Flashlight.
Panties from heaven.

Suddenly the subway
smells like roses.

Important to go in unprepared.
The peasantry in the basement. She looks at the crowd and
says,

"Another body
fed to the morning."

3
Brushed my hand
against the invisible dancer.

My hand brushed

by the invisible dancer.

But that's the one that you've already named.

Lost it.   Lost it.

XVII

Swallow flits through
the light   stars overhead   gross
leaves of the olive trees
a sluggish river

does not grow old   a hand
reaches, twists:

who knows the singer if he doesn't sing?

who reigned over the remains of from his balcony. The past
an eloquent shell.

The ceaseless hum of traffic.
The somnolent opaque river   reeds
near the shoreline pulled,
twisted by current.

Pulling it
homewards.

Reflections of light on stone
celebrate the youth's transparency.
Clench   release   flex.
Because the Second World War was about to begin.
Never lost, or
never found.

XVIII

Twitter of starlings,
gas tanks.

How many kinds of repetition.

The sign says "men
working in trees," so
the trees are full of men.

If a bat could soar
like a hawk, or even a swallow.

XIX

1
Eyes in the clouds for starlight.

I looked up
and there I was

penny arcade beyond the outhouse.

Night put
his children to sleep.

Then dream of turquoise.

2
Immortal anger
of the slave.

The demon chief.

The swallows will not feed their neediest child.

Who feeds the quail
now
that she has gone   who feeds them
for her?

3

You know if you're on the path.

Like a predator studying the weak points, looking for the

It had grown late. The river of images across the room had moved from football to comedies to old movies when he sprung the trap.

The tongue leaves no trace.

No light in the dead kitchen.

XX

Arbitrary flowers.

Enough song   to throw away
and still have plenty.

His history had worked his body.
Her other lovers had had no histories.

Something about the imagination of space.
Spontaneous collapse of a garden chair.

On a cloudy day
white sleep overtakes me.
In my dream
streetlights like sunflowers.

XXI

The one mosquito that spoils midnight.

Some kind of act of will.

Put down
as neatly as possible. The puddle
in my neighbor's rain-gutter
is green and black
green and black
shimmers with wind, and reflects
the leaves and branches.

A school kid passes   his radio,
rock and roll. Soon
just the drums in the distance.

XXII

Used to sing   but now I talk.
Take a walk.

Made up
to look bruised.

She was wearing a prosthetic leg in addition
to the two "normal"
ones that she already had

And was dancing the dance of

Break out and shout!

Biting the dead skin at the edge of his/her fingers.

Wondering what kind of blowjob the speaker gives, how her
hands
wrap themselves.

XXIII

Still sitting
as the room fills with women.
She turns to her friend.

Always clothes.
The eyelid's drapery.

Words. Who else
is there?

XXIV

1
Nostalgia for the franchise.
I had this insight:
a kind of weather
you never saw before.

Small shocks to the system.

She tosses, toss-
es, articulation of
bones and hair.
Bend your knees
brings it out in the open. A swift
motion, then gone.

Each thing
a gate
when the word
slips its

I could brush my teeth if you left me alone. I bend
to guide you down the stairs again. *If I bend my knees–*
then gone. A horse, a gazelle.

2
A scourge among the possums.
The goddess comes

in the form of a childish voice
reclining on the wind.

It could have fallen anywhere,
anybody's bird.

Turn to the light, she said, I've been trying
a long time now.

XXV

A fish looks up
decides to fly   but can't
it's not that kind
of fish.

.

Ocean   he said
has fish.

With fish in it.

XXVI

She swims to me
across the car seat.

And the night ends with a pearl tongue.

XXVII

I stay by myself   read little
make few choices.

Steady, limited men
in dark suits.

                    The boys
are leaving home   their girls
their trees
and the dark hills rising behind the house.

A forest with large blossoms,
large as grapefruit, and fulsome
to the point of rottenness.

XXVIII

1
We pay
extra
for sincerity.

The air ripe
with cat piss.

2
I have written a novel called "Fido's Revenge."

3
I stay by myself   read little
make few choices.

4
The idea
that one sensation
can be the latch-pin of memory.
The red-haired girl in the street
in a green scarf
braving the wind.

XXIX

We got stars
and a silver moon.

Some stars moving.

Dividing the plate into what will
and will not
be eaten.

Small words
big talk
lots of clarity.

Rhythm go broke.

What was
and will be
depopulates the prairie.

Outside the city walls
a prey to birds.

The shower of gold blown from the tree.

Segregation by foot-size.

A sideward glance

suspicious and curious
as in the Vermeer, and her skin,
her ear,
the small stone ornament.

Never doubted the dancing.

Across the field
faster than thought. "You choose the moves
and improvise."

When night came
I was glad night came.

I closed my eyes and had golden hair.

XXX

What had she said that night? "You're a baby." Grown-up stuff she had gotten out of books, out of the book of her anger.

Not to question the broken man's humility.

This is the rhetoric of meaning, the footstep–
imprint hardened.

Studying cartilage.

Square-headed she
of the russet pubic hair.

XXXI

for Gertrude Stein

"As if they liked it very well to live alone."

Sturdy
and strenuous.

Ordinary visions and trees. She sees
the heavenly city as a flock of pigeons
scattered in the yellow grass. To open your
eyes,
she says, how lovely
its accidents.

XXXII

The moon on a hubcap.

Stole the clapper from the sky-bell.

Who is my
he is my
where is my

XXXIII

Where old, as in
"the oldest this-or-that."

All that's cheap,
all that's tawdry.

The diamond's glint.

The ear's keyhole.

The hairless ridge behind the ear.

Not wanting to see her in a different context
because confused by that address
he'd never seen
in her. Is this
the girl I thought

Having no thoughts.

With a great prick like
the Priapus in the garden at Pompeii shown
with a leer to the tourist girls   what an ass
on that one, when she grows

to fullness

So disturbed by scent
that she wore nose-clips in public places.

XXXIV

Naked
in filthy water.

A license to wonder.

That row of trees beyond the ridge.

A florid portrait
a theatrical forest
a few pink irises.

The connoisseur of ears
the student of earlobes.

There's enough, he says,
but I'm not full.

Tell me that you saw no horrors today.

XXXV

Inhabiting
that body.

The child
who killed
itself
become a wound
that always festers.

XXXVI

1
Silent, because of windows.

2
Girls naked as rocks,
and in the forest there were three cautious deer.

Swim westward on the bed.

Each of our hands were jaws
with five sharp claws.

His leg's shadow staining her thighs.

3
The serpent's tongue divides the undergrowth.
Like kissing a flower.

Waiting for the girl to walk through the shadows of branches.

Suddenly that bare tree
was a burst of magnolia.

Even the weight of a bird could break this twig.

4
The old man.
The purveyor of ketchup.

When I was younger I wanted to live
a life without regrets.
I have invented
rindless bread
and other things, beside.

XXXVII

One flat blackbird sunning itself
in my still-bare pear tree
when the white-bellied flock of pigeons from across the yard
wheels through the bright blue sky.

The structure of static as individual as fingerprints.

Involved in seeing and hearing.

A black bird in a tree.

A black bird in a tree.

A black bird in a tree.

XXXVIII

Some say that strange and beautiful begin to play
between the summer and the savage wind.

Lady Springtime
steps heavily.

Birds sing,
eat bugs.
The context of happiness.

I imagine you come from the land of gourds,
gourds and melons everywhere.

What you call "misery" we call
"street theater."
Grateful for the small breeze. That's all
you get here, all you get.
Watching the light move across the shadow.

All the things your mother warned you of. All
her craziest fears.

XXXIX

Studying regret
I named three things,
this one, that
and t'other.

A rattle made of hands, the jingle
of tarsals and metatarsals.

The curve of narrative
a crescent moon.

Masks.
Faces, almost visible,
in the weave of the rug.

Move everything
to get rid of the shadow.

XL

White wrist
blue veins
rain on the mountains.